Everyday Expressions in Japanese

Junior Course of
Ono Japanese Class

by

Hideichi Ono

Assist. Professor of Tokyo University
of Foreign Studies

Lecturer at the Association for
Overseas Technical Scholarship

1963

THE HOKUSEIDO PRESS
TOKYO

First Printing August, 1963
34 th Printing September, 1990

ISBN 4-590-00211-6

Published by The Hokuseido Press
3-32-4, Honkomagome, Bunkyo-ku, Tokyo

FOREWORD

In the case of the mastering of the Japanese language, there are numerous words and expressions which are used according to the time and circumstances and also the position of the person to whom we are speaking or of the people referred to in the conversation. These numerous ways of speaking in Japanese can be definitely regarded as due to the fact that not only verbal terms but also the names of people and articles should respectively be varied, in keeping with their role or their purpose in regard to one's actions, the person concerned in the conversation, etc.

But, aside from such a fact as this in the mastering of Japanese, the author especially emphasizes the study of everyday wordings. This is because of the author's conviction that it is the shortest and the best way towards attaining a command of the conversation of any foreign language.

The Japanese letters, so complicated to write and memorize, might not induce foreigners to cherish the time they must devote themselves to study them. But foreigners might prove quite successful in achieving the conversation and understanding of the Japanese language without being confronted by any difficulties. Because in Japanese a great many words have no accent, the whole is pronounced in almost the same tone as in the English language. For instance, the word *asagohan* (breakfast) is not accented on any syllable. It is pronounced as *asa-go-han*. And in speaking Japanese, each tone should be

even, except when the sentence is marked with
an interrogative point. In this case, questions
are asked by adding the particle *ka* at the end
of the sentence—this *ka* is distinguished only
by the rising accent.

This is the book **Everyday Expressions in
Japanese—Junior Course of Ono Japanese Class
—**, which is written in a way by which the citi-
zens of all nations, not familiar with the Japanese
language, will be aided in daily practicalities—
this book, the author believes, has offered and
covered, in quite an easy approach for the foreigners, practically all the basic, common and
daily necessary expressions, words and phrases
that confront us in all ranks of life.

In this edition I have added, besides such a
section as common nouns of place, a simple ex-
planation of *numbering*, and *the post words*, char-
acteristic of the Japanese language.

In the author's opinion, it is desirable that
those foreigners who would further like to speak
and understand Japanese with a sound command
of its knowledge should learn carefully with the
book **Lessons in Japanese Conversation and Read-
ings—Senior Course of Ono Japanese Class—**.

Embracing the opportunity of this publication
I have to express my thanks to Mr. Junpei Naka-
tsuchi of the Hokuseidō Press for his kind help.

23rd July 1963

Hideichi   Ono

CONTENTS

I. Greetings and Common Everyday Expressions

(✓ means voice is raised a little on preceding vowel.)

SALUTATION

Good morning!	Ohayō gozaimasu.
Good afternoon!	Konnichi wa.
Good evening!	Kon-ban wa.
Good night!	Oyasumi nasai.
Good-bye!	Sayōnara.
So long!	Sayōnara.
Good luck!	Gokigenyō.
See you again.	Mata omeni kakarimashō (*or* Mata oaishimashō).
See you tomorrow.	Myōnichi omeni kakarimasu (*or* Myōnichi oai shimashō).
See you later.	Nochihodo omeni kakarimashō.
See you soon.	Chikaiuchi ni omeni kakarimasu.
Good-bye. And good luck!	Sayōnara odaiji ni.
Please take care of yourself.	Dōzo okarada o taisetsu (*or* odaiji) ni.
Good luck and a safe return (trip)!	Dōka ogenki de ittekite kudasai (*or* Gobuji ni).
We will pray for your success.	Goseikō o oinorishite orimasu.

Please give my thanks (regards; best wishes) to your wife also.	Okusan nimo yoroshiku.
Please give my love to your mother and everyone at home.	Okāsan o hajime mina-sama ni yoroshiku.
Well, I earnestly desire your continuing good health.	Dewa kureguremo oka-rada o taisetsu (*or* odaiji) ni.

ANSWERS AND RESPONSES EXPRESSING

(1)

Yes,	Hai,
No,	Iie⤴
Your name?	Onamae wa⤴
Your age?	Otoshi wa⤴
Your occupation?	Oshigoto wa⤴
Yes, it is.	Hai, sōdesu.
No, it is not.	Iie⤴ sōdewa arimasen.
No, not yet.	Iie⤴ mada desu.
No, not especially.	Iie⤴ betsuni.
Please.	Dōzo.
Well; Let me see.	Sōdesu ne; Sā.
Well, it's all right.	Mā īdeshō (*or* yoroshī-deshō).
All right.	Yoroshīdesu.
Certainly, I will.	Shōchi shimashita (*or* Kashikomarimashita; Yoroshīdesu).

Is that so?	Sōdesu ka⤻
Oh, I see.	Ā sō.
I see.	Sōdesu ne.
Then,	Soredewa.
Please do it for me.	Onegai shimasu.
That's a good idea.	Sore wa yoi kangae desu ne (*or* Sore wa i omoi-tsuki desu ne).
That's right.	Sōdesu (*or* Sono tōri desu).
After all,	Yappari (*or* Yahari; Tsumari; Kekkyoku).
Of course,	Mochiron.
Then, please do.	Dewa, dōzo.
Yes, you're right.	Hontōni sōdesu ne.
That's strange.	Sore wa okashī (*or* hen) desu ne.
That's possible.	Sōkamo shiremasen.
You know it, don't you?	Gozonji deshō⤻
Yes, I remember.	Hai, oboete-imasu.
No, I don't remember.	Iie⤻ oboete-imasen (*or* wasuremashita; wasurete-imasu).

(2)

I thank you.	Arigatō gozaimasu.
Thank you very much.	Dōmo arigatō gozaimashita (*or* gozaimasu).
Through your kindness,...	Okagesama de...

I sincerely thank you for your frequent help.	Itsumono kotodesu ga makoto (*or* hontō) ni arigatō gozaimasu.
Thank you very much for your kindness the other day.	Kono aida wa arigatō gozaimashita.
Today I'll take you down to Ginza in return for your kindness.	Kyōwa orei ni Ginza e otsure shimashō.
I'm much obliged to you for your generosity.	Korewa goteinei ni oso-reirimasu.

(3)

Please forgive me.	Gomen nasai.
Don't mention it.	Dō itashimashite.
There's no need to worry.	Shimpai wa irimasen.
I don't mind.	Kamaimasen.
I don't care.	Daijōbu desu yo (*or* Hei-kidesu).
I'm a little worried (uneasy).	Sukoshi shimpai desu.
I feel relieved.	Anshin shimashita.
Please set your mind at ease.	Goanshin kudasai.
It was a pity.	Okinodoku deshita.
I was surprised.	Bikkuri shimashita.
I'm overjoyed.	Ureshikute tamarimasen.
Please, don't forget anything.	Owasuremono no naiyō ni.

I'm sorry I'll be unable to attend today's meeting. Please forgive me.	Zannen desu ga kyō no kai niwa shusseki dekimasen. Ashikarazu.
I'm sorry to bother you, but...	Sumimasen ga...
I must apologize to you.	Owabi shinakereba narimasen.
I'm much obliged to you.	Dōmo osewasama desu.
Sorry to have caused you trouble.	Sumimasen deshita (*or* Otesū o okake itashimashita).

VISITS AND INTRODUCTIONS

What is your name?	Anata no onamae (*or* namae) wa nanto mōshimasu (*or* īmasu) ka⁄
May I ask your name?	Anata wa donata (*or* dare) desu ka⁄
My name is Ono.	Watashi wa Ono to īmasu (*or* Watashi no namae wa Ono desu).
May I see Mr. Ono?	Ono-san ni omeni kakaritai (*or* menkaishitai) no desu ga.
Where's your house?	Anata no ouchi (*or* otaku) wa doko desu ka⁄
Is Mr. Ono at home?	Ono-san wa gozaitaku (*or* ouchi) desu ka⁄
A visitor has come, sir.	Okyaku-sama ga omie ni narimashita (*or* Okyaku-san ga kimashita).

No, he is not at home.	Iie⸍ gofuzai desu (*or* Iie⸍ irasshaimasen; Iie⸍ imasen; Iie⸍ orusu (*or* rusu) desu).
I would like to call on you again to pay my respects.	Aratamete goaisatsu ni ukagaimasu (*or* agarimasu).
He has just gone out.	Chōdo odekake ni natta bakari desu (*or* Ima dekaketa bakari desu).
I'm going to visit you to-night.	Kon-ban anata no tokoro e ukagaimasu.
When will he be back?	Itsu okaeri ni narimasu ka⸍ (*or* Itsu omodori desu ka⸍).
He will soon be back.	Sugu modori (*or* kaeri) masu.
I don't have any special business.	Betsu ni yōji wa arimasen.
That's Mr. Ono's house, isn't it?	Ono-san no otaku desu ne.
I would like you to come tomorrow.	Asu (*or* Myōnichi; Ashita) oide kudasai.
I'll invite you to my home to-night.	Kon-ban (*or* Kon-ya) anata o goshōtai (*or* omaneki) shimasu.
Please tell me your name and address.	Namae to jūsho o oshiete kudasai.
Please wait here.	Kokode (*or* Sono mama) omachi kudasai.
Would you mind waiting for a while?	Chotto matte kudasaimasen ka⸍

Please wait just a moment.	Chotto matte kudasai.
Sorry to have kept you waiting.	Omatase shimashita.
Please come in.	Dōzo ohairi kudasai.
Please come in. I'll serve you tea. Please!	Oagari kudasai. Ocha o iremasu. Sā dōzo.
Hello! May I apologize for the other day?	Yā Kono-aida wa shitsurei shimashita.
Do come in!	Irasshai mase.
Please take off your shoes.	Dōzo okutsu o onugi kudasai (or Dōzo kutsu o nuide kudasai).
Please change to slippers.	Surippa ni hakikaete kudasai.
Please come this way.	Dōzo kochira e (or kochira e oide kudasai).
I'll show you into the reception room.	Ōsetsuma (or Ōsetsushitsu) ni goannai shimasu.
Please put on these slippers.	Kono surippa o ohaki kudasai (or haite kudasai).
It is here (It is there. There it is).	Koko desu (Asoko desu; Soko desu).
Not over there—here!	Sochira dewa-arimasen, koko desu.
Please be seated.	Okake nasai (or Dōzo okake (or osuwari) kudasai).
Sorry to have called on you without warning.	Totsuzen otazuneshite sumimasen (or Totsuzen ojamashite mōshiwake arimasen; Totsuzen ukagatte sumimasen).

Mr. Ono, I'm sorry to bother you so late.	Ono-san, yabun (*or* yoru) osoku ojamashite gomen nasai (*or* sumimasen).
Excuse my intrusion.	Dewa ojama itashimasu.
Thank you for taking the trouble to come.	Yoku irasshai mashita (*or* Yoku kite kudasai-mashita).
I apologize for not having come to see you for such a long time.	Gobusata o shimashita.
Ah, Mr. Ono! You really did come.	Yā (*or* Mā) Ono-san yoku kite kudasaimashita ne.
Please make yourself at home.	Dōzo oraku ni shite kudasai.
I'm pleased to meet you.	Hajimete omeni kakari-masu.
Mr. Tanaka, allow me to introduce to you Mr. Ono.	Tanaka-san, Ono-san o goshōkai shimasu.
How do you do!	Dōzo yoroshiku.
I'm very glad to meet you.	Omeni kakatte taihen ureshīdesu.
How do you do!	Dōzo yoroshiku (*or* Kochira koso).
Are you well?	Ogenki (*or* Ikaga) desu ka⌇
Are you all well?	Minasan ogenkidesu ka⌇
How is Yokohama?	Dō desu Yokohama wa.
How's the family there getting along?	Okawari wa arimasen desu ka⌇

Yes, thanks.	Hai, okage de (*or* Hai, okagesama de).
Yes, thanks. And you?	Ee okagesama de (*or* Arigatō gozaimasu). Genki desu. Anata wa⁄
You also seem to be well as usual.	Anata mo aikawarazu genki sōdesu ne.
Yes, I'm very well. Thank you.	Ee, genkidesu. Dōmo arigatō gozaimasu.
Yes, I'm well, so please don't worry.	Hai, genkidesu kara goanshin kudasai.
By the way, I've got something I want to talk with you about.	Tokorode sōdan (*or* ohanashi) ga arimasu.
I'm afraid I'll have to leave now.	Korede (*or* Mō) shitsurei shimasu (*or* shitsurei itashimasu).
Are you going home, sir?	Okaeri desu ka⁄
Please take your time (Please don't hurry).	Dōzo goyukkuri (*or* goyukkuri shite kudasai).
Give this message to Mr. Ono.	Ono-san ni kotozuke o onegai shimasu (*or* kotozuke o shite kudasai).
Have you a message for me?	Kotozuke ga arimasu ka⁄
Is there anything to attend to, sir?	Nani ka goyō desu ka⁄

AT TABLE

Oh, it's been a long time since I saw you last.	Yā hisashiburi (*or* shibaraku) desu ne.
Will you have a cigarette?	Tabako o dōzo.
May I have a cigarette?	Tabako o ippon itadakemasen ka͢
Are you hungry?	Onaka ga sukimashita ka͢
I'll take you to Ginza and treat you to dinner.	Ginza e sasotte (*or* otsureshite) yūshoku o gochisō shimashō.
Are you thirsty?	Nodo ga kawakimashita ka͢
Bring me a pot of tea (strong tea; weak tea).	Ocha (koi ocha; usui ocha) o kudasai.
I'll make black tea or something.	Kōcha demo iremashō.
I'll drink *sake*, with you for company.	Anata o aiteni *sake* o nomimashō.
Please bring coffee and cookies.	Kōhī to okashi o mottekite kudasai.
Please help yourself to an orange (an apple; some grapes; a persimmon; a pear).	Mikan (Ringo; Budō; Kaki; Nashi) o oagari (*or* otabe) kudasai; oagari (*or* tabe) nasai.
I'll try some of this (*or* Yes, I'll have some).	Itadakimasu.
Shall we have a cup of tea while we talk?	Ocha demo nominagara hanashimashō ka͢

Shall I heat some water for coffee?	Oyu o wakashite kōhī o nomimashō ka⟋
Shall I serve you tea?	Ocha o iremashō ka⟋
Will you pass the sugar (salt; pepper; mustard)?	Satō (Shio; Koshō; Karashi) o totte kudasaimasen ka⟋
How good this treat is! (or Say! This is good).	Gochisō desu ne.
Yes, thank you. Don't mind if I do.	Hai, arigatō gozaimasu. Enryo naku itadakimasu.
Please have another one.	Mō hitotsu oagari (or otabe) kudasai; oagari (or tabe) nasai.
Shall I bring you some more?	Mō sukoshi sashiage (or age) mashō ka⟋
May I ask for a second helping?	Okawari shitemo īdesu ka⟋ (or yoroshī desu ka⟋)
No, thank you. I've had enough.	Iie⟍, mō kekkōdesu.
Don't hesitate (Don't be polite).	Enryo shinaide kudasai (or Go-enryo naku).
No, I have really had enough.	Iie⟍, hontōni kekkōdesu.
Which would you like better, European or Japanese food?	Yōshoku to washoku to dochira ga osuki (or suki) desu ka⟋
I like European food better.	Yōshoku no hō ga suki-desu.
May I offer you some fish?	Osakana (or Sakana) wa ikagadesu ka⟋

Please serve me quickly.	Hayaku onegai shimasu.
That was delicious (or really good; a splendid meal).	Gochisō samadeshita (or Itadakimashita).
Give me the menu.	Kondatehyō (or Menyū) o misete kudasai.
Bring me the bill.	Kanjōgaki o kudasai.

INQUIRIES IN THE STREET

I don't know the way to the station.	Eki e iku michi ga wakarimasen.
Excuse me, officer.	Chotto ukagaimasu.
Which is the best way to get to the station?	Eki e iku niwa dō ittara īdeshō ka⌒
*Take this road to the left.	Kono michi o hidari e ikinasai.
*Turn that corner and go straight on.	Sono kado o magatte massugu ni irasshai.
How long does it take on foot?	Aruite dono kurai kakarimasu ka⌒
*Well, it will take about ten minutes.	Sōdesu ne jippun gurai kakaru deshō.
Please show me the way.	Michi o oshiete kudasai.
Where do you want to go?	Doko e oideni naritai (or Doko e ikitai) no desu ka⌒

---

* (Note that the speaker of the sentence is a person being questioned or a policeman, but never the inquirer.)

I'd like to tour a shipyard.	Zōsenjo o kengaku shitaidesu (or shitai no desu).
Please spread out a map of Tōkyō city.	Tōkyō tonai no chizu o hirogete kudasai.
What place is this?	Koko wa doko desu ka⁄
Is there a police stand around here?	Kono chikaku ni kōban ga arimasu ka⁄
Have you a guide map of Tōkyō city?	Tōkyō tonai no chizu o motte imasu ka⁄
Please show me on this map.	Kono chizu de shimeshite (or oshiete) kudasai.
Would you mind drawing a map on this paper?	Kono kami ni chizu o kaite kudasaimasen ka⁄
Isn't there any place where we can go?	Doko ka iku tokoro wa arimasen ka⁄
I'm going to take as many photographs as I can.	Ōini (or Takusan) shashin o torō to omotteimasu.
I think you probably know it.	Gozonji deshō.
Please write here (showing a slip of scratch paper).	Koko e kaite kudasai.
I intend to go sightseeing in Kyōto in a little while.	Chikai-uchini Kyōtokenbutsu ni iku tsumoridesu.
Can you guide me?	Annai shite itadakemasu ka⁄
Will you kindly interpret for me?	Tsūyaku o shite itadakemasen ka⁄

Would you kindly conduct me around Asakusa for sightseeing?	Asakusa o annaishite kudasaimasen ka⟋
I'd be glad to go with you.	Yorokonde otomo shimashō.
May I take your picture?	Anata no shashin o tottemo īdesu ka⟋
I will take you there.	Watashi ga annai itashimashō (*or* goannai shimashō).
Which is the way to the Imperial Palace?	Kyūjō (*or* Kōkyo) e iku michi wa dochira desu ka⟋
Will you come with me?	Isshoni mairimasen (*or* ikimasen) ka⟋
I'll take a picture of the Imperial Palace.	Kōkyo no shashin o torimasu.
Is it far (Is it near)?	Tōi desu ka⟋ (Chikai desu ka⟋)
Does this road lead to Ueno Park (a zoo; a museum; an art gallery; an aquarium)?	Kono michi wa Ueno kōen (dōbutsuen; hakubutsukan; bijutsukan; suizokukan) e ikimasu ka⟋
Please call a taxi.	Takushī o yonde kudasai.

SHOPPING, etc.

I'm going. (I'm leaving).	Itte mairimasu (*or* Itte kimasu).
Where are you going?	Doko e dekake (*or* iki) masu ka⟋

I'm going sightseeing around Tōkyō.	Tōkyō-kenbutsu ni ikimasu (*or* Tōkyō kenbutsu o shimasu).
I'm going to Mr. Ono's house to pay my respects.	Ono-san no otaku (*or* ouchi) e goaisatsu (*or* aisatsu) ni ikimasu.
Which way shall we go?	Dochira e mairimashō (*or* ikimashō) ka◞
Let's go shopping at Ginza.	Ginza e kaimono ni ikimashō.
Thank you for taking the trouble to go shopping (said beforehand).	Itte irasshai (*or* Itte irasshai mase).
Be careful. Finish your business and then return home.	Kiotsukete itte irasshai (*or* itte irasshai mase).
Please get ready to go out.	Dekakeru shitaku o shite kudasai.
I'm now getting dressed.	Ima shitaku o shite imasu.
Please wait until I come.	Watashi ga mairimasu (*or* kuru) made matte kudasai.
I can't wait.	Omachi dekimasen.
I'm in a hurry.	Watashi wa isoideimasu.
I'm making a trip to the Kansai district next month.	Rai-getsu Kansai-chihō e ryokō shimasu.
I should like to accompany you.	Otomo o itashimashō.
When does the train for Ueno start?	Ueno yuki no densha wa nanji ni demasu ka◞

Where is the train for Ginza?	Ginza yuki no densha wa dore desu ka✓
Is this the train for Ginza?	Kore wa Ginza yuki no densha desu ka✓
What is the next station, please?	Tsugi no eki wa doko desu ka✓
Is this an express?	Kore wa kyūkō desu ka✓
Where do we change cars for Ueno?	Ueno yuki wa doko de norikae desu ka✓ (or norikaemasu ka✓).
Please check the railroad timetable.	Kisha no jikan (or jikanhyō) o shirabenasai (or oshirabe kudasai).
Take me to Ginza. (to a taxi driver)	Ginza made itte kudasai.
How much will it cost?	Ikura desu ka✓
I'm going on a trip to Ōsaka in three days.	Mi-kka go (or ato ni) Ōsaka e ryokō shimasu.
How much for two singles (returns)?	Katamichi (Ōfuku) nimai de ikura desu ka✓
Where is a department store?	Hyakkaten (or Depāto) wa doko desu ka✓ (or Hyakkaten wa doko ni arimasu ka✓)
Where is the toilet (the post office; a barber shop; a restaurant; a theatre; a dance hall)?	Benjo (or Otearai; Gofujō; Senmenjo) (Yūbinkyoku; Tokoya; Shokudō; Gekijō; Dansu hōru) wa doko desu ka✓
Where can I buy a Japanese doll?	Doko de Nihon ningyō ga kaemasu ka✓

Where can I buy this? (showing a picture)	Doko de kore ga kaemasu ka⌣
Where should I go to buy this?	Kore o kauniwa doko e ittara īdesu ka⌣
Please come to Shinjuku Station by one o'clock.	Ichiji made ni Shinjuku eki e kite kudasai.
Let's go by subway.	Chikatetsu de ikimashō.
Is this a sightseeing bus?	Kore wa kankōbasu desu ka⌣
Where shall we meet at Shinjuku station?	Shinjuku eki no doko de machiawase (or machi) mashō ka⌣
Then, I hope you won't be late.	Dewa okurenaiyōni ne⌣
*Good afternoon, sir! (Welcome, sir!)	Irasshai mase.
*May I help you? (What can I do for you?)	Nani ni itashimashō ka⌣ (or Nani o omeni kakemashō ka⌣)
Show me a nice souvenir.	Nanika yoi omiyagemono o misete kudasai.
What kind would you prefer?	Donna noga yoroshīdeshō ka⌣
How much is this?	Kore wa ikura desu ka⌣
What price is this?	Kono nedan wa ikura desu ka⌣
It is too expensive.	Sore wa takasugimasu.

* (Note that the speaker of the sentence is the salesman, but never the customer)

It is expensive, isn't it?	Sore wa takaidesu ne.
Is there nothing cheaper?	Motto yasuinowa arimasen ka
*Please look closely.	Chotto otameshininatte goran nasaimase.
I will buy this.	Kore o kaimashō.
I will take it.	Sore ni itashimasu.
I'll buy flowers or something.	Hana demo kaimasu.
Is this of Japanese make?	Kore wa Nihonsei desu ka
Won't you reduce the price a little?	Sukoshi makari (or makerare) masen ka
*Today everything has a ten percent discount.	Kyō wa zenbu ichiwaribiki ni natteorimasu.
Please give me the change from one thousand yen.	Sen en de otsuri o kudasai.
Put the socks into a box.	Sono kutsushita o hako ni irete kudasai.
Wrap them, please.	Sore o tsutsumigami ni tsutsun de kudasai.
Please pack them.	Tsutsun de kudasai.
*Here is your change.	Kore ga otsuri de gozaimasu (or otsuri desu).
*Please count it (Please check it).	Dōzo oshirabe kudasai.

* (Note that the speaker of the sentence is the salesman, but never the customer)

I haven't any change now.	Ima otsuri ga arimasen.
*Haven't you anything smaller (small coins)?	Komakai okane ga arimasen (deshō) ka⟋
Please change this (Make change for this).	Dōzo kore o komakaku shite (*or* kuzushite) kudasai.
I will pay you now.	Ima (shi)haraimasu.
Here is my address.	Kore wa watashi no jūsho desu.
My address is...	Watashi no jūsho wa...
Here is my card.	Kore wa watashi no meishi desu.
Send them to this address.	Kono tokoro (*or* jūsho) ni todokete (*or* okutte) kudasai.
Send them to the International Students House.	Kono Ryūgakusei Kaikan ni todokete kudasai.
Let me have them in time.	Maniauyōni todokete kudasai.
When will it be ready?	Itsugoro dekimasu ka⟋
I'll call for it next Wednesday, so please have it ready.	Raishū no suiyōbi ni torini kimasu kara onegaishimasu.
I want to cancel the order.	Chūmon o torikeshimasu.
When will it be convenient for me to call on you?	Itsu ukagaimashitara yoroshīdesu ka⟋
When shall I come next time?	Kono tsugi wa itsu mairimashō ka⟋

I have much to attend to.	Takusan yōji ga arimasu.
I must get back by two o'clock.	Niji made ni modoranakereba narimasen.
I'm back!	Tadaima.
I've just returned.	Tadaima kaerimashita.
Welcome home. (back).	Okaerinasai.
Thank you for your trouble.	Gokurōsama deshita.

TELEPHONES, etc.

Have you no telephone at home?	Otaku ni denwa ga arimasen ka⌇
Can I make a call from here?	Koko de denwa o kakeru kotoga dekimasu ka⌇ (or Koko de denwa ga kakeraremasu ka⌇)
Will you permit me to use your 'phone?	Osoreirimasu (or Sumimasen) ga denwa o kashite kudasai.
What number do you want to call?	Nanban e okake ni naritai nodesu ka⌇ (or Nanban e kakemasu ka⌇)
Hello.	Moshi moshi.
Hello, is this Fujimae 941–6091?	Moshi moshi, Fujimae no kyū yon ichi no roku zero kyū ichi ban desu ka⌇
I'm sorry to bother you, but could you call Mr. A to the telephone?	Sumimasen ga A-san o denwa ni onegaishimasu.

Mr. A, there's a telephone call.	A-san denwa desu (*or* A-san denwa desu yo).
Will you please get me this number?	Kono bangō o yonde kudasai masen ka⁄
Where is the telephone?	Denwa wa doko ni arimasu ka⁄
Whom is it from?	Dare (*or* Donata) kara desu ka⁄
It's from a man named Ono.	Ono-san to iū hito kara desu (*or* Ono-san to iū kata kara desu).
It's from a foreigner.	Gaikokujin (*or* Gaijin) kara desu.
Can you speak Japanese?	Anata wa Nihongo ga hanasemasu ka⁄
Yes, I can.	Hai, hanasemasu.
Yes, I can speak it a little.	Hai, sukoshi hanasemasu.
No, I cannot.	Iie⁄, hanasemasen.
You are good at Japanese, aren't you?	Anata wa Nihongo ga jōzudesu ne.
No, I'm still poor at it.	Iie, mada hetadesu.
I can't say anything difficult.	Muzukashī koto wa hanasemasen.
This is Ono speaking.	Watashi wa Ono desu.
Can you hear me?	Kikoemasu ka⁄
I can not hear you.	Kikoemasen.
I will call you back.	Atode kakemasu.
I don't know the other party's number.	Senpō no denwabangō ga wakarimasen.

Please look it up in the telephone directory.	Denwachō de shirabete kudasai.
Line is busy.	Ohanashi chū desu.
Long distance, please.	Shigaidenwa o onegai-shimasu.
Please hang up the receiver and wait.	Juwaki o oite omachi kudasai.
Take off the receiver.	Juwaki o hazushinasai.
Put in a ten yen coin.	Jūen dama o irenasai.
No connection is made.	Tsunagarimasen.
Where is a public telephone booth?	Kōshūdenwa wa doko ni arimasu ka⁄
Where is the telephone directory?	Denwachō wa doko ni arimasu ka⁄
There's the telephone!	Denwa ga kakatte ki-mashita (or Denwa desu).
It was a call from home.	Jitaku (or Uchi) kara denwa ga kakatte ki-mashita (or Uchi kara denwa deshita).

EXPRESSIONS OF JOY AND ANGER

I'm very interested in Japan's culture.	Nihon no bunka (or Nihon bunka) ni kyōmi ga arimasu (or kyōmi o motte-imasu).
I'm satisfied (dissatisfied) with my life in Japan.	Nihon no seikatsu ni manzoku (fuman) desu (or manzokushite-imasu (fuman de-imasu).

I've become accustomed to Japanese daily conversation.	Nihongo no nichijō kaiwa ni naremashita (*or* narete-imasu).
I've lost interest in the study of Japanese.	Nihongo no benkyō ni akimashita (*or* akite-imasu).
The study of Japanese is very interesting (uninteresting).	Nihongo no benkyō wa taihen (*or* hijōni) omoshiroi desu (omoshiroku arimasen).
I'm tired from my long journey.	Nagai tabi (*or* ryokō) de tsukaremashita (*or* tsukarete-imasu).
I'm looking forward to seeing you again.	Anata tono saikai o tanoshimi ni shite-imasu.
At last I feel at home in Japan.	Yatto Nihon no seikatsu ni naremashita.
I don't want to make a nuisance of myself to you.	Anata ni gomeiwaku o okakeshitaku arimasen (*or* meiwaku o kaketaku arimasen).
Life (*or* Living) in Japan bores me.	Nihon no seikatsu wa tsumaranai desu.
I've become despondent.	Yūutsu ni narimashita (*or* Yūutsu ni natte-imasu).
He treats me kindly.	Shinsetsu ni shite kuremasu.
He is very kind to me.	Watashi ni taihen shinsetsu desu.
Ah! This is wonderful (experience).	Subarashī keiken desu.

It's really pleasant (unpleasant).	Hontō ni tanoshī desu (fuyukaidesu).
I'm having a very good time.	Tanoshiku sugoshite-imasu.
I'm thinking that I would like to make an inspection tour of Japan.	Nihon o shisatsushitai to omotte-imasu (*or* kan-gaete-imasu).
I feel lonely because I haven't any Japanese friends.	Nihonjin no tomodachi ga inai node sabishī desu.
I'm truly embarrassed because even now I can't handle Japanese daily conversation well.	Ima demo Nihongo no nichijō kaiwa ga yoku dekinai (*or* hanasenai) node hontōni komari-masu (*or* komatte-imasu).
I feel a longing for my home town.	Kokyō ga koishiku nari-masu (*or* Kokyō ga koi-shī desu).
The beautiful change of seasons in Japan delights my heart.	Utsukushī Nihon no shi-ki no henka ga watashi o tanoshimasete (*or* yo-rokobasete) kuremasu.
Foreigners appreciate the rarity of Japanese stamps.	Gaijin wa Nihon no kitte o mezurashigarimasu.
Japanese Kimono is a novelty to foreigners.	Nihon no Kimono wa gaijin ni mezurashī desu.
My hobby is collecting *Kokeshi* (a kind of Japanese doll).	Watashi no shumi wa *Kokeshi* no shūshū desu.
I always feel refreshed.	Itsumo ī kimochi desu.

I'll stifle my emotions.	Kanjō o osaemasu.
I have no grief.	Shimpai ga arimasen.
There's no need to be ashamed.	Hazukashiku wa arimasen (or Hazukashigaru hitsuyō ga arimasen).
I like (dislike) Japan.	Nihon ga suki (kirai) desu.
I don't know too much about life in Japan.	Nihon no jijō (or yōsu) ga yoku wakarimasen.
I can't recall his face.	Kare no kao ni oboe ga arimasen (or Kare ni mioboe ga arimasen).
Japan's customs and manners are quite different from those in my country.	Nihon no fūzoku shūkan wa watashi no kuni to taihen chigaimasu (or chigatte-imasu).
Don't get angry with me.	Okora (or Hara o tate) naide kudasai.
Yesterday I was scolded by the manager.	Kinō shihainin (or manejā) ni shikararemashita.
It's no concern of mine.	Watashi niwa kankei ga arimasen.
This scenery is wonderful!	Kore wa subarashī keshiki da!
I feel a surge of anger.	Hara ga tachimasu.
I'm happy (unhappy).	Kōfuku (Fukō) desu.
I'm lucky (unlucky).	Kōun (Fuun) desu.
I'm pleased (sad).	Ureshī (Kanashī) desu.
I feel sorry for him.	Kawaisō (or Kinodoku) ni omoimasu (or omotte-imasu).

What impressed you most?	Dono ten ni inshō zuke-raremashita ka‿
That work of art greatly impressed me with its elaborateness.	Ano seikō na kōgeihin ni tsuyoi inshō o ukema-shita (or ukete-imasu).
She gives me an impression of cleanliness.	Kanojo wa seiketsu na kanji ga shimasu (or Kanojo wa seiketsu na inshō o ataemasu).
She is generous (reserved; faithful; docile; obedient).	Kanojo wa kandai (hika-eme; chūjitsu; sunao; jūjun) desu.
She laughs (weeps).	Warai (Naki) masu.
He is a cheerful (gloomy) man.	Yōki (Inki) na hito desu or Akarui (Kurai) hito desu.

WEATHER FORECASTS

It is warm.	Atatakai desu.
It is very hot.	Taihen atsui desu.
It is becoming warmer day by day.	Higoto ni (or Mainichi mainichi) atatakaku nat-te kimasu.
It is cold.	Samui desu.
You're chilly, aren't you?	Samukatta deshō.
It was a little cool last evening.	Yūbe sukoshi samukatta desu.
It rains.	Ame ga furimasu.
It is raining heavily.	Ame ga hidoku futte-imasu.

It looks as if it will rain.	Ame ga furisō desu.
The light rain continues.	Ame ga shito shito to furitsuzukimasu.
The rain of the night before seems to have cleared.	Sakuya kara no ame mo agatta yōdesu.
Tōkyō, where it looks like rain (or Tōkyō, where it looks like it will rain)	Ame moyoi no Tōkyō.
It stops raining.	Ame ga furiyamimasu (or yamimasu).
The weather is quite disagreeable.	Iyana tenki desu.
It has turned out fine.	Ii (or Yoi) tenki (or otenki) ni narimashita.
Ah! It's fine weather.	Ā, yoi (or ii) tenki (or otenki) da.
The rain prevented me from going there.	Ame ga futte soko e ikemasendeshita.
If it rains, I'll stay away from the company.	Ame ga fureba kaisha o yasumimasu.
It snows.	Yuki ga furimasu.
The wind blows.	Kaze ga fukimasu.
The wind died down.	Kaze ga yowaku narimashita.
It is very windy.	Kaze ga tsuyoku fukimasu (or kaze ga hidoi (or tsuyoi) desu).

It is a windy evening.	Kaze no fuku ban desu.
On top of the rain, the wind began to blow, too.	Ame ga furu ueni kaze mo fukidashimashita.
The outskirts of Tōkyō are quiet, and the air is refreshing.	Tōkyō no kōgai wa shizuka de kūki mo suga suga shīdesu.

II. The Pronunciation of Numbers

CARDINAL NUMBERS

0. rei (*or* zero)	10. jū (*or* tō)
1. ichi (*or* hitotsu)	11. jū-ichi
2. ni (*or* futatsu)	12. jū-ni
3. san (*or* mittsu)	13. jū-san
4. shi; yon (*or* yottsu)	14. jū-shi (*or* jū-yon)
5. go (*or* itsutsu)	15. jū-go
6. roku (*or* muttsu)	16. jū-roku
7. shichi; nana (*or* nanatsu)	17. jū-shichi (*or* jū-nana)
8. hachi (*or* yattsu)	18. jū-hachi
9. ku; kyū (*or* kokonotsu)	19. jū-ku (*or* jū-kyū)

20. ni-jū (*or* futa-jū)	60. roku-jū
30. san-jū	70. shichi-jū (*or* nana-jū)
40. shi-jū (*or* yon-jū)	80. hachi-jū
50. go-jū	90. ku-jū (*or* kyū-jū)

100. hyaku (*or* ippyaku)	600. roppyaku
200. ni-hyaku (*or* futa-hyaku)	700. shichi-hyaku (*or* nana-hyaku)
300. san-byaku	800. happyaku
400. shi-hyaku (*or* yon-hyaku)	900. ku-hyaku (*or* kyū-hyaku)
500. go-hyaku	

1,000. sen (*or* issen)	7,000. shichi-sen (*or* nana-sen)
2,000. ni-sen (*or* futa-sen)	8,000. hassen
3,000. san-zen	9,000. ku-sen (*or* kyū-sen)
4,000. shi-sen (*or* yon-sen)	10,000. man (*or* ichi-man)
5,000. go-sen	
6,000. roku-sen	

105. hyaku-go
250. ni-hyaku-go-jū
397. san-byaku-kyū-jū-shichi
                            (nana)
4,005. yon-sen-go
4,020. yon-sen-futa-jū (*or* yon-sen-ni-jū)
4,471. yon-sen-yon-hyaku-nana-jū-ichi

COUNTING AGES

1	year	old	issai (*or* hitotsu)
2	years	old	ni-sai (*or* futatsu)
3	//	//	san-sai (*or* mittsu)
4	//	//	shi-sai; yon-sai (*or* yottsu)
5	//	//	go-sai (*or* itsutsu)
6	//	//	roku-sai (*or* muttsu)
7	//	//	shichi-sai; nana-sai (*or* nanatsu)
8	//	//	hassai (*or* yattsu)
9	//	//	ku-sai; kyū-sai (*or* kokonotsu)
10	//	//	jissai (*or* tō)
11	//	//	jū-issai (*or* jū-ichi)
12	//	//	jū-ni-sai (*or* jū-ni)
13	//	//	jū-san-sai (*or* jū-san)
14	//	//	jū-shi-sai (*or* jū-yon)
15	//	//	jū-go-sai (*or* jū-go)
16	//	//	jū-roku-sai (*or* jū-roku)
17	//	//	jū-shichi-sai (*or* jū-nana)
18	//	//	jū-hassai (*or* jū-hachi)
19	//	//	jū-ku-sai (*or* jū-kyū)
20	//	//	ni-jissai (*or* hatachi)
30	//	//	san-jissai (*or* san-jū)
40	//	//	shi-jissai (*or* yon-jissai); shi-jū (*or* yon-jū)
50	//	//	go-jissai (*or* go-jū)
60	//	//	roku-jissai (*or* roku-jū)
70	//	//	shichi-jissai (*or* nana-jū)
75	//	//	shichi-jū-go-sai (*or* nana-jū-go)

COUNTING PEOPLE, BIRDS, ...

People

1	2	3	4	5
hito-ri	futa-ri	san-nin	yo-nin	go-nin
(ichi-nin)	(ni-nin)			

Birds

ichi-wa	ni-wa	san-ba	shi-wa	go-wa
			(yon-ba)	

Animals

i-ppiki	ni-hiki	san-biki	shi-hiki	go-hiki
			(yon-hiki)	

Long articles (pencils, poles, etc.)

i-ppon	ni-hon	san-bon	shi-hon	go-hon
			(yon-hon)	

Thin objects (sheets of paper, dishes, etc.)

ichi-mai	ni-mai	san-mai	yon-mai	go-mai

books

i-ssatsu	ni-satsu	san-satsu	yon-satsu	go-satsu

Pairs of shoes, socks, etc.

i-ssoku	ni-soku	san-zoku	shi-soku	go-soku
			(yon-soku)	

Glasses (**cups**) of water, drink, etc.

i-ppai	ni-hai	san-bai	shi-hai	go-hai
			(yon-hai)	

Doses of medicine

i-ppuku	ni-fuku	san-puku	yon-puku	go-fuku

Houses

i-kken	ni-ken	san-ken	yon-ken	go-ken

Floors of building (Ordinal numbers are the same as for **Times** except "san-gai")

i-kkai	ni-kai	san-gai	yon-kai	go-kai

Vehicles (taxis, buses, bicycles, etc.)

| ichi-dai | ni-dai | san-dai | yon-dai | go-dai |

Furnitures & machines (tables, desks, beds, telephones, etc.)

| ichi-dai | ni-dai | san-dai | yon-dai | go-dai |
| i-kkyaku | ni-kyaku | san-kyaku | yon-kyaku | go-kyaku |

(for **Chairs**, etc.)

Ships

| i-sseki | ni-seki | san-seki | yon-seki | go-seki |

Boats

| i-ssō | ni-sō | san-sō | yon-sō | go-sō |

Boxes, cartons, cases, etc.

| hito-hako | futa-hako | mi-hako | yon-hako | go-hako |
| | | (san-bako) | | |

Clothes (a suit of foreign clothes, a pair of trousers, etc.)

| i-cchaku | ni-chaku | san-chaku | yon-chaku | go-chaku |

Things in general

| i-kko | ni-ko | san-ko | yon-ko | go-ko |
| or hitotsu | futatsu | mittsu | yottsu | itsutsu |

Times or occasions

| i-kkai | ni-kai | san-kai | yon-kai | go-kai |
| or ichi-do | ni-do | san-do | yon-do | go-do |

COUNTING MONEY

1 yen	ichi-en		100 yen	hyaku-en
2 //	ni-en		200 //	ni-hyaku-en
3 //	san-en		300 //	san-byaku-en
4 //	yo-en		400 //	yon-hyaku-en
5 //	go-en		500 //	go-hyaku-en
⋮			⋮	
10 //	jū-en		1,000 //	sen-en
20 //	ni-jū-en		2,000 //	ni-sen-en
30 //	san-jū-en		3,000 //	san-zen-en
40 //	yon-jū-en		4,000 //	yon-sen-en
50 //	go-jū-en		5,000 //	go-sen-en

10,000	yen	ichi-man-en
20,000	//	ni-man-en
30,000	//	san-man-en
40,000	//	yon-man-en
50,000	//	go-man-en
374	//	san-byaku-nana-jū-yon-en
		(yo)
1,540	//	sen-go-hyaku-yon-jū-en
7,005	//	nana-sen-go-en
23,400	//	ni-man-san-zen-yon-hyaku-en
		(futa-)

TWELVE MONTHS OF THE YEAR AND THE FOUR SEASONS

January	ichi-gatsu	September	ku-gatsu
February	ni-gatsu	October	jū-gatsu
March	san-gatsu	November	jū-ichi-gatsu
April	shi-gatsu	December	jū-ni-gatsu
May	go-gatsu	Spring	haru
June	roku-gatsu	Summer	natsu
July	shichi-gatsu	Autumn	aki
August	hachi-gatsu	Winter	fuyu

THE DAYS OF THE MONTH

1st	tsuitachi	9th	kokono-ka
	(*or* ichi-jitsu)		(*or* ku-nichi)
2nd	futsu-ka	10th	tō-ka
3rd	mi-kka	11th	jū-ichi-nichi
4th	yo-kka	12th	jū-ni-nichi
5th	itsu-ka	13th	jū-san-nichi
	(*or* go-nichi)	14th	jū-yo-kka
6th	mui-ka	15th	jū-go-nichi
	(*or* roku-nichi)	:	

7th	nano-ka	20th	hatsu-ka
	(*or* shichi-nichi)		(*or* nijū-nichi)
8th	yō-ka	21st	nijū-ichi-nichi
	(*or* hachi-nichi)		⋮

THE DAYS OF THE WEEK

Sunday	nichi-yōbi	Thursday	moku-yōbi
Monday	getsu-yōbi	Friday	kin-yōbi
Tuesday	ka-yōbi	Saturday	do-yōbi
Wednesday	sui-yōbi		

ORDINAL HOURS & QUARTERS OF THE DAY

1 o'clock	ichi-ji	A. M.	gozen
2 //	ni-ji	P. M.	gogo
3 //	san-ji	2 P. M.	gogo ni-ji
4 //	yo-ji	8 A. M.	gozen hachi-ji
5 //	go-ji		

morning	asa	(To express the half-hour
noon	hiru	the word "han" is used:
evening	ban	6 : 30 roku-ji han)
night	yoru	

COUNTING DAYS, YEARS, MONTHS, etc.

Days (hi)

1 day	ichi-nichi	9 days	ku-nichi	
2 days	ni-nichi		(*or* kokono-ka	
	(*or* futsu-ka(-kan))			(-kan))
3 //	san-nichi	10 //	tō-ka(-kan)	
	(*or* mi-kka(-kan))	11 //	jū-ichi-nichi	
4 //	yo-kka(-kan)	12 //	jū-ni-nichi	
5 //	go-nichi	13 //	jū-san-nichi	
	(*or* itsu-ka(-kan))	14 //	jū-yo-kka	

6 days	roku-nichi	15 //	jū-go-nichi
	(or mui-ka(-kan))	:	
7 //	shichi-nichi	20 //	nijū-nichi
	(or nano-ka(-kan)		(or hatsuka
8 //	hachi-nichi		(-kan))
	(or yō-ka(-kan))	21 //	nijū-ichi-nichi

Years (toshi)
ichi-nen, ni-nen, san-nen, yo-nen, go-nen, ...
(14 years jū-yon-nen or jū-yo-nen; jū-shi-nen)

Months (tsuki)
i-kkagetsu, ni-kagetsu, san-kagetsu, yon-kagetsu, ...
(hito-tsuki) (futa-tsuki) (mi-tsuki) (yo-tsuki)

Weeks (shū)
i-sshūkan, ni-shūkan, san-shūkan, yon-shūkan, ...

Hours (jikan)
ichi-jikan, ni-jikan, san-jikan, yo-jikan, ...

Minutes (fun)
i-ppun, ni-fun, san-pun, yon-fun, ...

Seconds (byō)
ichi-byō, ni-byō, san-byō, yon-byō, ...
(yo-byō; shi-byō)

PRESENT, PAST, FUTURE
(genzai, kako, mirai or shōrai)

today	kyō
this morning	kesa
this noon	kyō no hiru
this afternoon	kyō no gogo
this evening	kyō no yūgata or kon-yū
to-night	kon-ban, kon-ya
yesterday	kinō, sakujitsu
yesterday morning	kinō no asa

yesterday noon	kinō no hiru
// afternoon	kinō no gogo
last night	yūbe, sakuban, **sakuya**
the day before yesterday	i-ssakujitsu, ototoi
tomorrow	ashita, asu, myōnichi
tomorrow morning	asu no asa, myōchō
// noon	asu (ashita *or* myōnichi) no hiru
// afternoon	asu no gogo
// night	asu no yoru, myōban
the day after tomorrow	asatte, myōgonichi
this week	kon-shū
last week	sen-shū
next week	rai-shū
(the next week	tsugino shū)
this month	kon-getsu, kono tsuki
last month	sen-getsu
next month	rai-getsu
(the next month	tsugino tsuki)
this year	ko-toshi
last year	kyo-nen
next year	rai-nen
(the next year	tsugino toshi)

ORDINAL NUMBERS

1st, No. 1	dai-ichi,	ichi-ban(-me),	ichi-gō
2nd, // 2	dai-ni,	ni-ban(-me),	ni-gō
3rd, // 3	dai-san,	san-ban(-me),	san-gō
4th, // 4	dai-yon,	yon-ban(-me),	yon-gō
5th, // 5	dai-go,	go-ban(-me),	go-gō
⋮	⋮	⋮	⋮	⋮
1st time	i-kkaime,	ichi-dome	
2nd //	ni-kaime,	ni-dome	

3rd time	san-kaime,	san-dome
4th //	yon-kaime,	yon-dome
5th //	go-kaime,	go-dome

1st hour	ichi-jikan-me
2nd //	ni-jikan-me
3rd //	san-jikan-me
4th //	yo-jikan-me

1st day	sho-nichi	7th day	nano-ka-me
2nd //	futsu-ka-me	8th //	yō-ka-me
3rd //	mi-kka-me	9th //	kokono-ka-me
4th //	yo-kka-me	10th //	tō-ka-me
5th //	itsu-ka-me	11th //	jū-ichi-nichi-me
6th //	mui-ka-me	12th //	jū-ni-nichi-me

1st year	ichi-nen-me	3rd year	san-nen-me
2nd //	ni-nen-me	4th //	yo-nen-me

1st class	i-ttō	3rd class	san-tō
2nd //	ni-tō	4th //	yon-tō

FRACTIONS

$1/2$	ni-bun no ichi		
$1/3$	san-bun no ichi	$2/3$	san-bun no ni
$1/4$	yon-bun no ichi	$3/4$	yon-bun no san
$1/5$	go-bun no ichi	$2/5$	go-bun no ni
$1/10$	jū-bun no ichi	$1/100$	hyaku-bun no ichi

PERCENTAGE

1 %	ichi-bu,	ichi-pāsento
2 %	ni-bu,	ni-pāsento
10 %	ichi-wari,	ji-ppāsento
20 %	ni-wari,	niji-ppāsento

III. Personal Pronoun

	Nominative		Possessive		Objective
(I)	watashi -wa, -ga*	(my)	watashi-no	(me)	watashi -o, -ni*
(you)	anata "	(your)	anata-no	(you)	anata "
(he)	kare "	(his)	kare-no	(him)	kare "
(she)	kanojo "	(her)	kanojo-no	(her)	kanojo "
(we)	watashi-tachi "	(our)	watashi-tachi-no	(us)	watashi-tachi "
	(wareware ")		(wareware-no)		(wareware ")
(you)	anata-tachi "	(your)	anata-tachi-no	(you)	anata-tachi "
	(anata-gata ")		(anata-gata-no)		(anata-gata ")
(they)	karera "	(their)	karera-no	(them)	karera "
	kanojora "		kanojora-no		kanojora "
(who?)	**donata ga	(whose?)	donata-no	(whom?)	donata "
	(dare ga)		(dare-no)		(dare ")

* See pp. 45-48. Note : -wa, -ga, -o, -ni, etc.

** 'Donata' is more polite than 'dare'.

IV. Family Relations

Plain (humble)	Honorific
(*my father*) watashi-no chichi	(*your (his, her) father*) anata-no (kare-no, ka- nojo-no) otōsan
(*my mother*) watashi-no haha	(*your mother*) anata-no okāsan
(*my parents*) watashi-no ryōshin	(*your parents*) anata-no goryōshin
(*my husband*) watashi-no shujin watashi-no otto	(*your husband*) anata-no goshujin anata-no danna-sama (*or* anata-no danna-san)
(*my wife*) watashi-no tsuma watashi-no kanai	(*your wife*) anata-no okusan
(*my elder brother*) watashi-no ani	(*your elder brother*) anata-no onīsan
(*my younger brother*) watashi-no otōto	(*your younger brother*) anata-no otōtosan
(*my elder sister*) watashi-no ane	(*your elder sister*) anata-no onēsan
(*my younger sister*) watashi-no imōto	(*your younger sister*) anata-no imōtosan
[*my brothers (or sisters)*] watashi-no kyōdai	[*your brothers (or sisters)*] anata-no gokyōdai
(*my son*) watashi-no musuko	(*your son*) anata-no musukosan

(*my daughter*)
watashi-no musume

(*your daughter*)
anata-no musumesan
(*or* anata-no ojōsan)

(*my grandfather*)
watashi-no sofu

(*your grandfather*)
anata-no ojīsan

(*my grandmother*)
watashi-no sobo

(*your grandmother*)
anata-no obāsan

(*my uncle*)
watashi-no oji

(*your uncle*)
anata-no ojisan

(*my aunt*)
watashi-no oba

(*your aunt*)
anata-no obasan

(*my nephew*)
watashi-no oi

(*your nephew*)
anata-no oigo-san

(*my niece*)
watashi-no mei

(*your niece*)
anata-no meigo-san

(*my cousin*)
watashi-no itoko

(*your cousin*)
anata-no itoko-san

(*my relatives*)
watashi-no shinseki

(*your relatives*)
anata-no shinseki no
kata (*or* anata-no go-
shinseki)

(*my family*)
watashi-no kazoku

(*your family*)
anata-no kazoku no kata
(*or* anata-no gokazoku)

(*my friends*)
watashi-no tomodachi

(*your friends*)
anata-no otomodachi

V. Verbs for Clothing Articles

	Put on (dress) 1. Action 2. The state of wearing...	Take off (undress)
(*a coat*) uwagi	1. kimasu 2. kite-imasu	nugimasu
(*trousers*) zubon	1. hakimasu 2. haite-imasu	nugimasu
(*socks*) kutsushita	1. hakimasu 2. haite-imasu	nugimasu
(*a cap*) bōshi	1. kaburimasu 2. kabutte-imasu	nugimasu (*or* torimasu)
(*shoes*) kutsu	1. hakimasu 2. haite-imasu	nugimasu
(*a necktie*) nekutai	1. shimemasu (*or* shimasu) 2. shimete-imasu (*or* shite-imasu)	hazushimasu
(*glasses*) megane	1. kakemasu 2. kakete-imasu	hazushimasu (*or* torimasu)
(*gloves*) tebukuro	1. hamemasu 2. hamete-imasu	torimasu (*pull off*)
(*a ring*) yubiwa	1. hamemasu 2. hamete-imasu	nukimasu (*take off*)

Comparable verbs:

(*an electric light*) dentō	1. tsukemasu (*switch on*) 2. tsukete-arimasu. (*or* tsuite-imasu)	keshimasu (*switch off*)
(*an umbrella*) kasa	1. sashimasu (*put up*) 2. sashite-imasu	subomemasu (*close*)

VI.   Adjectives of Quality and Feelings, Antonyms, and Adverbs

Adjective	Antonym	Adverbial Form	
wide hiroi	*narrow* semai	*widely* hiro**ku**	*narrowly* sema**ku**
deep fukai	*shallow* asai	*deeply* fukaku	*shallow* asaku
long nagai	*short* mijikai	*longly* nagaku	*shortly* mijikaku
big ōkī	*small* chīsai	*largely* ōkiku	*small* chīsaku
high takai	*low* hikui	*highly* takaku	*lowly* hikuku
cold samui	*warm* atsui	*coldly* samuku	*warmly* atsuku
light karui	*heavy* omoi	*lightly* karuku	*heavily* omoku
strong tsuyoi	*weak* yowai	*strongly* tsuyoku	*weakly* yowaku
thick atsui	*thin* usui	*thickly* atsuku	*thinly* usuku
fast (or *early*; *quick*) hayai	*slow* (or *late*) osoi	*fast* hayaku	*slowly* (or *late*) osoku
black kuroi	*white* shiroi	*black* kuroku	*white* shiroku
soft yawarakai	*hard* katai	*softly* yawarakaku	*hard* kataku
new atarashī	*old* furui	*newly* atarashiku	*formerly* furuku
glad ureshī	*sad* kanashī	*gladly* ureshiku	*sadly* kanashiku

dark	bright	darkly	brightly
kurai	akarui	kuraku	akaruku
convenient	*inconvenient*	*conveniently*	*inconveniently*
benrina	fubenna	benrini	fubenni
kind	*unkind*	*kindly*	*unkindly*
shinsetsuna	fushinsetsu-na	shinsetsuni	fushinsetsu-ni
happy	*unhappy*	*happily*	*unhappily*
kōfukuna	fukōna	kōfukuni	fukōni
cheerful	*gloomy*	*cheerfully*	*gloomily*
yōkina	inkina	yōkini	inkini
skilful	*unskilful*	*skilfully*	*unskilfully*
jōzuna	hetana	jōzuni	hetani
honest	*dishonest*	*honestly*	*dishonestly*
shōjikina	fushōjikina	shōjikini	fushōjikini
clever	*foolish*	*cleverly*	*foolishly*
rikōna	bakana	rikōni	bakani
diligent	*lazy*	*diligently*	*lazily*
kinbenna; majimena	fumajimena; funesshinna	kinbenni; majimeni	fumajimeni; funesshinni
fortunate	*unfortunate*	*fortunately*	*unfortunately*
kōunna	fuunna	kōunnimo	fuunnimo
reasonable	*unreasonable*	*reasonably*	*unreasonably*
seitōna	futōna	seitōni	futōni
sufficient	*insufficient*	*sufficiently*	*insufficiently*
jūbunna	fujūbunna	jūbunni	fujūbunni
quiet	*noisy*	*quietly*	*noisily*
shizukana	urusai; yakamashī	shizukani	urusaku; yakamashiku
accurate	*inaccurate*	*accurately*	*inaccurately*
seikakuna	fuseikakuna	seikakuni	fuseikakuni
necessary	*unnecessary*	*necessarily*	*unnecessarily*
hitsuyōna	fuhitsuyōna	hitsuyōni	fuhitsuyōni
complete	*incomplete*	*completely*	*incompletely*
kanzenna	fukanzenna	kanzenni	fukanzenni

VII. Honorific Forms of Verbs for Giving and Receiving

(A) Kyōju ga watashi ni kono hon o kudasaimashita. (*The professor gave me this book*).

Kudasaimashita is the past form of the verb kudasaru (Polite Form), to give—it is used when a superior or an equal does some favor for someone, while kuremashita is the past form of the verb kureru (Plain Form) and means that a subordinate or an equal does a favor, in almost all cases, for those whom he is closely connected with. Note that the subject of the sentence is somebody else, but never the speaker.

(B) Watashi wa kono hon o sensei ni agemasu. (*I'll give this book to the teacher.*)

Agemasu comes from the verb ageru (Polite Form), to give—it is used when the speaker or the subject of a sentence does a favor for an equal or a superior, while yaru, the plain form of the verb ageru, is used when doing a favor for a subordinate or an equal—one of your own family members, close friends, or children.

(C) Watashi wa kono shinju o haha kara itadakimashita. (*I received this pearl from Mother.*)

Itadakimashita is the past form of the verb itadaku (Polite Form)—it is used when the subject of the sentence is given some gift from an equal or a superior, while morau, (its past tense being moraimashita) the plain form of the verb itadaku, is used when being given some gift from a subordinate or an equal.

VIII.   Important Japanese "Particles"

The difference between "-wa" and "-ga"

"-wa" is used for denoting nominative case such as in simple statements in English. "wa" follows the subject immediately, and is used when the predicate, not the subject, is emphasized.

"-ga" is used when the subject of the sentence is comparatively or specially emphatic.

Yama *wa* takaidesu (The mountain is high).

Yuki *ga* furimasu (It snows).

For answers to a question "Dare ga kono shigoto o shimashita ka" (Who did this work?)

Watashi *ga* shimashita (I did).

Watashi *wa* shimasendeshita (I did not).

When the negative form is used, the subject as a rule is followed by "wa".

"ga" following verbs

Yuki wa furu *ga* samuku arimasen (It snows but it is not cold).

This "ga" shows the condition of paradox.

Kanojo wa kao wa utsukushī *ga* sugata wa utsu-kushiku arimasen (Her face is beautiful, but her form is not beautiful).

This "ga" shows contrast. This corresponds to "but" in English. The "wa" in this sentence following "kao" and "sugata" is used because this sentence is a contrast of two ideas and thus the subject of each idea takes special emphasis. The "wa" following "kanojo" indicates the subject of the entire sentence.

Watashi mo mita *ga* totemo subarashikattadesu
(I myself saw it, which, I found, was splendid).

This "ga" shows a slight connection,—the preceding word or sentence acts upon the following as a mere succession.   This nearly corresponds to "and" in English.

"o"

1. "o"—an objective particle—"o" follows the direct object immediately.

   Anata wa kyō no gogo nani *o* shimasu ka?
   (What will you do this afternoon?)

   Watashi wa Tōkyō Tawā *o* mimasu
   (I see Tōkyō Tower).

2. "o" denotes a place where or through which an action occurs.

   Watashi wa Ginza *o* samposhimasu.
   (I take a walk along the Ginza).

   Chikatetsu wa tōri no shita *o* hashitteimasu.
   (The subway is running under the street).

   "o" sometimes takes the same role as *kara* (from) in meaning.

   Watashi wa seki *o* hanaremasu.
   (I'll leave my seat).

   Watashi wa densha *o* orimasu.
   (I get off the electric car).

"ni"

1. "ni"—Denoting a Place of Existence—the place of existence is followed by "ni."

   Koko *ni* Indo no gakusei ga go nin imasu
   (There are five Indian students here).   (existence)

cf. Indo no gakusei ga kono Nihongo gakkō *de* Nihongo o benkyōshiteimasu
(Some Indian students are studying Japanese at this Japanese language school). (*de* denotes a place of action; that is, it refers to the place where an action is performed).

2. "ni" follows the indirect object immediately.

Watashi wa Indojin *ni* Nihongo o oshiemasu
(I teach Indians Japanese).

3. to express the time of action.

Anata wa kesa nan ji *ni* okimashita ka?
(What time did you get up this morning?).

4. "ni" designates purpose.

Watashi wa eiga o mi *ni* ikimasu
(I'll go to see a movie).

5. quasi-adjectives used adverbially are followed by "ni."

Anata wa sugu Nihongo no nichijōkaiwa ga jōzu *ni* narimasu
(You'll soon be good at Japanese daily conversation).

6. agent of passive action indicated by "ni."

America wa Columbus *ni* hakken saremashita
(America was discovered by Columbus).

7. agent of causative action indicated by "ni."

Sensei wa gakusei *ni* shi o tsukurasemasu
(The teacher makes the students compose poems).

*"de"

1. denotes means or instrument.

Watashi wa hikōki *de* Nihon e kimashita
(I came to Japan by plane).

Watashi wa kare o kenjū *de* koroshimashita
(I killed him with a revolver)

2. the place of action is followed by "de".

Watashi wa koko *de* kanojo ni aimashita
(I met her here).

*"e"

1. denotes a direction.

Anata wa doko *e* ikimasu ka?
(Where do you go?)

cf. Watashitachi wa asa roku ji ni mokutekichi *ni*
tsukimashita
(We arrived at our destination at six o'clock in
the morning).

"ni" expresses a point and corresponds to the English "in" or "at". "e" expresses a direction and corresponds to the English "to" or "toward".

IX.   Common Nouns of Place

The Ministry of Finance	Ōkurashō
The Ministry of Agriculture and Forestry	Nōrinshō
The Welfare Ministry	Kōseishō
The Ministry of Transportation	Unyushō
The Labor Department	Rōdōshō
The Ministry of Construction	Kensetsushō
The Office of Attorney General	Hōmushō
The Ministry of Education	Monbushō
The Ministry of Postal Services	Yūseishō
The Foreign Office	Gaimushō
The Ministry of Trade and Industry	Tsūsanshō
*a radio station	hōsōkyoku
a police station	keisatsusho
a police stand	kōban
a telephone office	denwakyoku
a telegraph office	denshinkyoku
the custom house	zeikan
a school	gakkō

---

* In Japanese there is no difference in form between singular and plural.

a church	kyōkai
a movie theatre	eigakan
American Embassy	America Taishikan
American Consulate	America Ryōjikan
a cafe	kafē
a concert hall	ongakudō
The Imperial Theatre	Teikoku gekijō
The Kabuki Theatre	Kabukiza
the baseball park	yakyūjō
a castle	shiro (*or* oshiro)
Nagoya Castle	Nagoya jō
Ōsaka Castle	Ōsaka jō
Hibiya Park	Hibiya kōen
The Yasukuni Shrine	Yasukuni jinja
Wrestling at Kokugikan	Kokugikan no sumō
The Meiji Shrine	Meiji Jingū
The Great Image of Buddha	Daibutsu
The Entrance Bridge of the Imperial Palace	Nijūbashi
Tōkyō Station	Tōkyō eki
Ueno Station	Ueno eki
Akasaka Detached Palace	Akasaka rikyū
a hospital	byōin
a dental office	haisha (*or* shikai)
a cigar store	tabakoya
a photographer's	shashinya
an art shop	bijutsuten

a curio-shop	kottōya
a jeweller's	hōsekishō
a watch-maker's	tokeiya
an optician's	meganeya
a music store	gakkiten
a book store	honya
a pharmacy	kusuriya
a foreign goods shop	yōhinten
a shoe-shop	kutsuya
a stationer's	bunbōguten
a hat-shop	bōshiya
Japanese wooden shoe-shop	getaya
a green-grocer's	yaoya
a tailor	yōfukuya
a confectioner's	kashiya
a dry goods store	gofukuya
a hardware store	kanamonoten
a rice shop	komeya
a florist's	hanaya
a fruit store	kudamonoya
a printing shop	insatsuya
a hotel	ryokan (*or* hoteru)
The Imperial Hotel	Teikoku hoteru
a boarding house	geshukuya
a foreign hotel	yōfū no hoteru
a Japanese hotel	nihonfū no hoteru (*or* ryokan)

the Immigration Bureau	Iminkyoku
the National Diet	Kokkai gijidō
the Kyōto Imperial Palace	Kyōto gosho
the Asahi newspaper	Asahi shimbun
the Association for Overseas Technical Scholarship	Kaigai gijutsusha kenshū kyōkai
a temple	otera
a shrine	jinja
a coffee (*or* tea)-house	kissaten
a cemetery (*or* a grave yard)	bochi
a tourist city	kankōtoshi
a recreation area	yūenchi
a botanical garden	shokubutsuen
a public lavatory	kōshū benjo
a day nursery	takujisho
old peoples' homes	yōrōin
the Ueno National Western Art Gallery	Ueno kokuritsu seiyō bijutsukan
noted places and historic sites	meisho kyūseki
beautiful scenic spots	keshiki no yoi tokoro
an astronomical observatory	tenmondai
a national park	kokuritsu kōen
a hot-spring	onsen
an old battle-field	kosenjō

a factory	kōjō
a city office	shiyakusho
a town office	murayakuba
a ward office	kuyakusho
a bank	ginkō